A HANDFUL OF SEEDS

by

Helen M. Downs

Published by

MELROSE BOOKS

An Imprint of Melrose Press Limited
St Thomas Place, Ely
Cambridgeshire
CB7 4GG, UK
www.melrosebooks.com

FIRST EDITION

Copyright © Helen M. Downs 2008

The Author asserts her moral right to
be identified as the author of this work

Cover designed by Helen M. Downs

ISBN 978-1-906561-02-4

All rights reserved. No part of this publication may be reproduced,
stored in a retrieval system, or transmitted, in any form or by any means
electronic, mechanical, photocopying, recording or otherwise,
without the prior permission of the publishers.

This book is sold subject to the condition that it shall not,
by way of trade or otherwise, be lent, re-sold, hired out or
otherwise circulated without the publisher's prior consent
in any form of binding or cover other than that in which
it is published and without a similar condition including this
condition being imposed on the subsequent purchaser.

Printed and bound in Great Britain by:
CPI Antony Rowe, Chippenham, Wiltshire

TABLE OF CONTENTS

Foreword? Forward!. 1
So You're a Skeptic Eh?. 3
Dimensions. 6
Auras & Chakras 10
The Energy System & Alternate Healing Therapies 15
Religion 18
Reality 21
Synchronicities, Intuition & Coincidences. 27
Fairies, Ghosts & Other Weird & Ooky-Spooky Things . . .31
Astral Travel. 38
Orbs 41
Body, Mind, Emotions 49
Meditation, Yoga, Tai Chi & the Like 57
Palmistry, Astrology, Numerology & Tarot 62

TABLE OF CONTENTS (cont.)

Angels, Guides & Guardians 67
Extraterrestrials – Is there Life out There?. 72
The Law of Attraction 83
So What about God?. 88
Earth Changes & our Future. 91

FOREWORD? FORWARD!

Our view of this earth and our reality has evolved over time and is still changing. There are those who are right "into" the New Age and/or ancient traditions and have intricate knowledge and understanding of specialized fields in energy, tone, vibration, spirituality and healing. **This book is not for them!** This book will not be likely to tell them anything they have not already heard, seen, done or worked with.

This book is for their friend, the skeptic, who silently wonders what weird and wacky flight of fancy they are on now. It is for those of you who would like to get a basic rundown that might possibly satisfy your very rational mind, or at least give you a clue as to where your "mung beans and dolphins" friends are coming from.

This book does not purport to have in-depth specialized information about anything in particular, but serves as a simple *guide and reference for anyone who would like to know or understand a bit more about the greater reality around us. Consider it as a handful of seeds, for concepts that might take root and grow in your thoughts over time. It gives several references to other works which I have found to be helpful in understanding these arenas. Most of the works referred to are succinct and informative or at least make for an interesting reading (or viewing) experience. As you read this, please, relax, keep an open mind and most of all ENJOY this composite guide to worlds beyond!*

Dedicated to dear Bison, who encouraged me "write it all down".

SO YOU'RE A SKEPTIC EH?

WHEN YOU DRIVE through the city and look at all the people going about their business, do you wonder what they think life is all about? I do constantly. I look at men in suits, strutting their self-important egos with their briefcases, mobile phones and ear attachments, women with stylish shoes and handbags, looking good, sporting stick-on fake fingernails painted to perfection, as if that's all that's important.

This book is not about all that. It is about the thing that ticks away inside us, the elusive sense of satisfaction that people seek, but only some find. It is about asking why many of us cannot, for a moment, believe in or entertain the *possibility* that crop circles are real, races from other planets exist, or that we might have something called a "soul" or a "spirit" that lives in dimensions larger than our own 3D world.

Some people religiously go to church and declare their

belief in the afterlife, Jesus' healing miracles and the angels, but are aghast if someone says they spoke to God or to their Guardian Angels, or can heal with their hands, or see or speak to the dead. Do you get the irony?

Some scientists are constantly sending probes and messages into space hopefully to find intelligent life, or extraterrestrial water molecules, while ignoring the countless stories of UFO contact in our own backyards, or worse, labelling such stories as obvious fiction and the work of crazy-people fit for white straight-jackets.

Does it not strike anyone as a little *odd* that we are so inclined to put our heads in the sand over so many things that don't fit our neat little paradigms, rather than looking openly at the countless unexplained phenomena that point solidly in the direction of something bigger than us?

Does it not seem eerily convenient that the majority of the world is locked into a pattern of disbelief and unwilling to prise open the corners of their minds for even just a second?

World leaders feed us bull by the barrel load and we trust in their wisdom, while declaring all politicians to be liars and cheats anyway.

We drive around in oil-fuelled cars and are at the mercy of the latest Middle Eastern tension, while never for more than a moment wondering why no one had a problem with big companies buying up all the hokey ideas by hokey mad inventors who came up with alternative power sources for cars, houses and machinery.

In short, worldwide, we are ruled by a handful of very rich people, who run very big companies, with agendas that in no way reflect our best interests or those of our delicate ecology (unless purely by chance or to help keep us complacent)... And we put up with it and shout down rebels who try to rise up and educate us as if they are riff-raff and mental cases. Why is that? Don't you ever think it's a little strange?

In this compilation, we take a look at a number of phenomena and ask if they are actually strange and unexplained, or if we just haven't been looking in the right places to understand them better. We seek to reintroduce some personal autonomy in our belief systems and learn to have more power over our own destiny and wellbeing.

DIMENSIONS

THE RIGHT PLACE to start is perhaps an understanding of the concept of dimensions. It is said that we live in a three dimensional world. We have a solid 3D shape. We are not flat, like 2D drawings. We are not a one-dimensional pinpoint. We have depth. If you lived in a 2D world and existed as a flat shape, a 3D being could only be perceived by you as the flat cross section plane that intersects your arena. Your understanding would be limited to that point of view, unless you were educated to know better.

What if, living as we are in 3D (or 4D if you count time as an extra dimension through which we are moving) a being of larger dimensions were to interact with us? Would we perceive them in totality, or would we just see the 3D "shadow" of their full self?

I ask this, not to introduce a full scientific exploration of the theme, but just as a point to ponder. Who says that 3D is as big as it gets? And what is their authority to say so? Why would we limit ourselves automatically to this basic foundational belief in our lives just because others say it is all there is?

Many books have been written exploring the dimensions beyond the third. Many wise and scholarly people have studied these realms and reported their findings. If you choose not to look at or explore these things yourself, are others to believe what you believe, just so that you all feel more comfortable living in the box of thought that seems safe and secure?

Surely not! It is said that knowledge is power, yet many will gladly avoid knowledge on many "strange" subjects, because they have been lulled by peer pressure to laugh at, ridicule, or ignore knowledge of how things actually work. They are quite "happy" to spend endless hours working in a dreary job they don't enjoy, to have a "life" where they can maybe, for two days out of seven, do something that feels a little more free and fun and once in a while take a holiday to enjoy a whole week or two at a time relaxing. Is this what life is all about? If you were a 5D Being, would you still choose this option?

The point about dimensions at this stage is that it's in your best interests at least to *explore* those greater than the one you live in. There are many learned men and women who have realized that *reality is not created in the third dimension* and for years they have been writing books and telling us how we can see it differently and create our preferred world with this knowledge.

Have you ever looked at one of those "Magic Eye" pictures? The ones that look like a bunch of squiggly lines and shapes with no meaning, until you go a little cross-eyed and look at them in a different way? Suddenly you see a picture in 3D leap off the page at you ... It's *so* 3D you have to poke it with your finger to see if it has depth. Suddenly you can see something where nothing of sense was there before, simply by looking at it differently. Life is like this too!

There is a story told about Magellan the explorer (or Columbus, depending on your source) but basically the story is the same. I will quote the story as told in the book *Preparing for Contact* by Lyssa Royal and Keith Priest:

> *"The Earth explorer Magellan visited a remote island, inhabited by native people. He anchored his big-masted ship out at sea and came to the island with his men in small row boats. When they arrived, the natives met them. Even though they saw the men rowing toward shore in the small boats, they couldn't see where those boats came from. It looked as if the boats came from nowhere.*
>
> *Magellan tried to explain that he came from a large masted ship that was anchored offshore. The natives could not see this ship. The reason for this was that in their reality construct, they had no previous information that would allow for that type of object in their reality. They could allow for the rowboats because they looked like their own canoes, but the masted ship did not fit into their view of reality.*
>
> *Magellan's men talked to the shamans of this society. Through work with the imagination and through repeated description of the sailing ship, the shamans were eventually able to see it anchored out at sea. On the day they could begin seeing the ship, it was as if*

A Handful of Seeds

a blindfold had been removed. They were astounded. Then the shamans' responsibility was to translate the information about this ship to the natives. The concepts for this ship anchored at sea had to be given to the villagers through several people repeatedly through time before the entire population could see it."

What you can or cannot see all depends on your reality construct and how you look at things. No amount of trying to prove the existence of a 5th or higher dimension will work if a person is only willing to look through 3rd dimensional eyes. You have no doubt heard many times that we are using only 10% of our brains' capacity. In this book, you are encouraged to keep your mind open and look beyond what you think you have always seen, to find glimpses of something the mind may not entirely grasp, but the senses may well perceive. You may find you have been perceiving it all along!

Turn to the pages 46 and 47 of this book for two examples of 3D pictures.

Suggested Magic Eye® Viewing Instructions

MAGIC EYE® 3D INSTRUCTIONS: Hold the center of the image *right up to your* nose. The image should be blurry. *Stare* as though you are looking through the image into the distance. *Very slowly* move the image away from your face until you begin to see depth. Now hold the book still, try not to blink, and a 3D image will magically appear! The longer you look, the clearer the illusion becomes.
© 2008 Magic Eye Inc.

AURAS & CHAKRAS

ONE OF THE things people often poke fun at is the idea that others can see auras: the emanations of light around the body of all living things. Yet there are those (not just a few) who grew up seeing them and never questioned nor were made to deny what they saw. We can bag those people and say they're fruitcakes, or we might want to see if there's something that *they* know that *we* don't.

Kirlian photography has been around for quite some time now. This is a kind of photography where scientists using an energy sensitive camera have taken pictures of flowers, leaves, fingers and other living things, and the pictures show emanations of light around the subject matter. Anyone who has seen a dead body can see how in the absence of this energy animating the body, the face and the muscles, all that is left is a lifeless shell without the persona it carried before.

The aura is simply the energy that animates us, radiating out like electricity in a light bulb, or the hum of a computer when it is switched on. It has a measurable field and some people can actually see it. Just because you can't, doesn't mean it doesn't exist. Ignorance of natural law is no excuse!

Further, while some people can see the aura, others can alternatively, or also, feel it. So can you. Try walking into the space of an angry person in an elevator and tell me you are oblivious to a feeling of tension or discomfort. Try sitting with a sick person for a time and tell me you don't feel drained or tired in their presence. Sure you can put this down to other logical factors ... or you can entertain for a moment that yes, you too might be sensing something beyond what the eyes can see or the mind can grasp.

There are those who not only sense the aura, but can direct their own energy, or a Higher energy, to that aura to bring it healing and balance. These people are not using some primitive witchcraft. They are working with the nature of things from a higher viewpoint than most of us perceive. In days of old they might have been burned at the stake as witches, because their persecutors could not or would not widen their own limited understandings. Surely by now, for instance, even YOU realize that the Earth is *not* flat and that it *does rotate* around the Sun. Times change and our understandings grow and enlarge.

Putting it very simply, the aura is fed by a number of *Chakras* (or "Energy Wheels") within and around the body. These chakras are points at which different "levels" of energy are focused in the body. You may want to think of them as "distribution points", similar to those in electricity supply from the mains to the wall plug.

Each correlates with its own specialized area in the body's energy system. There are various methodologies which count from five to thirteen or more chakras, but most often the main ones, more popularly acknowledged, are seven in number. Often, those who meditate will focus on each of the chakras and visualize them clear and spinning, to unblock or amplify feelings of general wellbeing.

The most commonly recognized chakras are as follows:

Starting at the base (perineum) of the body, and said to draw Earth energy up from the planet we live on, is the "Base", or "Root" Chakra. This chakra is traditionally associated with the colour red, and corresponds with issues of our basic survival and connection to life on a material level.

Next is the genital chakra, situated in the lower abdomen. It is associated with the colour orange and corresponds with our emotional needs and feelings.

Above this, situated in the solar plexus area, is the third or solar plexus chakra. It is associated with the colour yellow and the concept of our sense of self as an individual.

Moving upwards again, the heart chakra is the centre for our feelings of love and connection with the outside world. Its colour is green.

The fifth chakra is the throat chakra, located (can you guess?) ... in the throat. It relates to our ability to communicate our truth and express ourselves. The colour of this energy centre is blue.

Next up, the third eye chakra, which is in the mid forehead region above and between the eyes. This relates to our higher vision, clairvoyant sight and conceptualizing. This chakra is associated with the colour range of indigo/purple/violet, depending on the system under which you are learning.

At the top of the head, above the middle of the skull, is the seventh or crown chakra, which is coloured white. It relates to our connection with the universe, our spirit and higher wisdom.

The whole aura itself is regarded as a chakra in some systems, such as that of the Druids. In their system, the aura is the tenth chakra and there are others between the points listed above.

As you can see, the colours corresponding with the chakras range up the spectrum as they do in a rainbow. In this regard, we are like prisms that contain all aspects of "cosmic light" within us (whether we can perceive them or not). Other (some more minor) points are found on the hands and feet, the shoulders and at other points around and outside of the body.

The function of these chakras is to step up or down the energy of the body's whole system. If there is imbalance in the system, it is usually because of a blockage or a "hole" in one or more of the chakras.

Those wishing to study in even more depth can acquaint themselves with the meridians, or lines of energy running around and through the body. These are primarily used in Chinese/Daoist–based systems, such as acupuncture.

The Druids and others also perceive similar lines of energy, running through the Earth and pinpointed at certain spots, perhaps the best known of which is Stonehenge.

In Earth terms, these lines of energy tend to coincide with places where more "phenomena" occur, such as ghost sightings or crop circles. They are places where the Earth energy is stronger or more focused and where ancient cultures would choose to perform rituals and ceremonies because of the enhanced qualities to be experienced there.

Suffice to say in general, energy moves in pathways, and centres both around the Earth and around in our bodies and there are fields of learning and understanding that map these pathways for our greater understanding.

THE ENERGY SYSTEM & ALTERNATE HEALING THERAPIES

IN THE SAME way as a city's electrical system is wired, with main connection points, power lines, ancillary connections and individualized terminals, so too is the body (and the Earth).

Western medicine tends not to acknowledge these energy lines and connections and consequently misses out on some levels of deeper understanding in relation to the formation and treatment of illness and disease. Some medical practitioners are starting to learn more about Eastern practices and incorporating this knowledge into their treatments for better results.

There is an ex NASA scientist named Barbara-Anne Brennan, who has pioneered some of the healing work in the West, using the chakras. In her book *Hands of Light* she shows examples of treatments working directly on the chakra points, rather than by surgical operations or pharmaceuticals, with successful results.

In the East, various forms of hands-on healing have been employed for centuries. The Chinese Daoist tradition is perhaps the oldest of such systems of practice. It is from the Daoist tradition that such well-known ancient studies as Tai Chi, Herbal Medicine, Acupuncture and Acupressure (to name just a few), were created. The Chinese have spent many centuries learning about and using the body's energy to successfully treat and understand imbalances and their treatment.

I mention these things to make you aware that more exists out there than the limited concepts and practices we were brought up to think of as "all there is to it". When Western medicine says that something is incurable, take the time to investigate reputable alternative therapies, as they may have answers based on different, but effective approaches.

Many people are so fixed in their mindsets that they cling only to the "rational", "logical" methods of pure science and medicine. Effectively, they would rather die, suffer enduring pain, or be continuously medicated, than look outside their limited and fixed belief system for a cure or a remedy.

Are you one of these people, and if so why? Are you embarrassed that someone might think you are weird? What does that say about your sense of self and autonomy, your ability to learn, discover and make decisions for yourself?

Do yourself a favour and allow yourself to step out of the dark ages of limited thought into the realm of a wider and truer reality, in keeping with the nature of things as they really are, beyond our limited perception.

A NOTE OF CAUTION

As in everything, there are good practitioners and there are ones to avoid. Whether you are considering healing from an alternative therapist, or even getting a reading from a clairvoyant, astrologer, or some other practitioner, be sure to find one who is acting with correct intent and a spiritual foundation.

The workings of energy are, in part, natural gifts arising from natural laws, but they need to be developed with a pure heart and wise intent.

There are many who, while having talents and abilities in these fields, are blatantly using them for self-serving, commercial purposes, or with less than true intent.

There are charlatans who may seek to make you dependant upon them and their services, rather than helping to educate you to maintain and improve your own wellbeing. There are also those who act without an ethical (self-imposed) code of practice and can bring more upset and dependency than relief or assistance. Such people have contributed largely to the general fear, mistrust and misunderstanding held by the populace towards alternative practices.

More will be said on this topic and on alternative therapies generally in later chapters, but in short, apply the same common sense in your dealings as you would, for instance, when purchasing a used car from a dealer, or a "genuine" Rolex watch at a market.

RELIGION

OK, SO WE'D better deal with this issue early in the piece. Many religions will preach that what is written here is some form of blasphemy or evilness at work; that these ways of looking at things are somehow inconsistent with a true belief in God and the Bible, and that God will not smile upon you if you read one line more of this book!

Search your own heart for answers on this. *Please!* Ask *God* what *He* thinks. If you are true to yourself, you may find that while your faith is tested, there is nothing I am saying that is actually inconsistent with the teachings of Jesus, or the true meaning of the Commandments. Fundamentalist churches may have you believe otherwise, but they *do* have something of a vested interest in maintaining your obedience to their set, limited belief structures. (Although I am referring specifically to Christian religions here, the same principle applies to any of the world's denominations.)

Senses and dimensions beyond our known basic ones are as much a creation of God as everything else is. He is unlimited. Do you think His vast eternal intention can be limited by earthly words and accounts in any one book?

You need to *feel* the sense of the teachings, not just their literal translation. (On that point, students of the Bible might want to be honest with themselves about the many passages and references that have been cut from the original texts over the centuries ... references to reincarnation, and respect for women, to name a couple. These were excluded in years long gone as they threatened the power of the Churches over their flock.)

No one can deny the original loving intent of religion, but you need to look earnestly and search hard within your truest of hearts to feel whether you actually wish to stand by every word and interpretation that is thrust upon you, whether it be by the Church, the Bible or by other devotees ... (or me for that matter).

People who quote the Bible to attack the ideas expressed herein, should take a leaf out of their own book and *"Judge not, lest ye yourself be judged"*.

God gave us Free Will on purpose. If we are to learn, grow and evolve, we need to be free to exercise that Will in accordance with our conscience and our truest beliefs that are found in our own hearts, where God is said to dwell. In fact, it could be said that our truest and deepest Will is that of God anyway.

I mean no disrespect to any devout churchgoer, and I implore you only to feel what is right privately between you and God.

Once you decide, that is your right and I withdraw from any attempt to further convince you of anything you don't want to hear.

That having been said, religion has a lot of inconsistencies within its practice. When was "Thou shalt not kill" reinterpreted to mean that the majority of wars and deaths on this planet would be caused by fervent religious beliefs being defended or thrust upon others in the name of God?

If God is omniscient and omnipresent, then how can *anything* not be His creation? And how can He not be found in ALL things, including your own heart of hearts, and mine? Is it not *we* who label things evil by declaring them so – judging them?

We are each entitled to our preference and on the whole, we tend to prefer peace, love and joy; but is that to say that God didn't create other points of view for a reason? Perhaps to cause us, through suffering, pain, or confusion, a glimpse of higher realizations, truer wisdoms, and deeper depths, through our experience of the great diversity of Life and Creation in all its forms? How many times has a message of truth only been learned after some mishap or disaster has befallen us?

Are the many religions and beliefs not just many aspects of the one God? How can they be otherwise?

Why won't we just all accept our Oneness – unite, and work together ... or alternatively give each other our own space, allowing each other the freedom to worship or not, in our own way, or at our own peril, as long as we harm no one? Isn't this what true Free Will, compassion and love are about?

Like I said, I'll leave it up to you. Whatever you decide is your decision, your path, your journey, your unique experience and not my choice (or anyone else's) to make for you.

REALITY

IF YOU HAVEN'T seen the movie *What the Bleep do We Know?* you should hire it out some time and have a look. In it there are a number of quantum physicists and others who expound the view and the scientific finding that we are creating our own realities as we go.

This is consistent with the teachings of the Spiritual Masters over the centuries and now scientists are showing it to be empirical fact.

They say that multidimensional existence is a reality and that we, through our choices, thoughts and feelings, are determining how we experience our world and our life – creating it for ourselves according to our attitudes and responses to things.

A good illustration of this principle is in an experiment conducted with sound. A group of metal filings are placed on a sheet and then a tuning fork is struck and held so that its sound vibrates against the filings.

It was found that for each different note, or tone, the filings arranged themselves into patterns, like snowflake formations and stars, in response to the different vibrations. The principle at work here is that material reality is being shaped by tone and vibration.

If you go back to our discussion on the aura and our energy, you'll recall that we too have an energetic vibration, which emanates from each of us. Depending on the tone of that emanation, the situations and creations that manifest around us in our physical world will be shaped accordingly.

In this way, our three dimensional reality is being created at levels above and beyond the third dimension. This is why it serves us to become aware of this natural truth and learn to work with it.

Some simplistic examples: A person with a pessimistic viewpoint who resonates such a tone will tend to have situations around them that justify this view. They are always being thwarted and disappointed – seemingly attracting those very situations again and again. A person who is continuously fearful will find there are many things to fear. A person who emanates strength may feel unaffected by the very same circumstances.

The shape of our personal experience is determined by the mindset and emotions we emanate with our personal energy.

In the early 20th century a woman named Florence Scovel-Shinn wrote a series of books, including one called *The Game of Life and How to Play It.* In it, she describes the process by which we create our reality, using the power of our words ... the tone we are setting and manifesting with the power of sound – exactly as when God *spoke the word* and there was Light!

Her books are well worth reading, as they explain quite simply how faith and the spoken word are so essential in the formation of our preferred experiences.

Sound, the words we choose to use, the vibration and tone we emanate, the beliefs we hold and resonate – these are the foundations of what we create in our lives. That is why so many have written at length about the power of positive affirmations: they are there both to remind us of the tone and belief we wish to create and also to bring that tone into manifest reality using sound as the medium.

Doctor Masuro Emoto, author of *Hidden Messages in Water* and *The True Power of Water,* made some interesting and fundamental findings in his experiments.

Photographs were made of water crystals, formed of water taken from various sources. The crystals that appeared were either harmonious and beautiful, or broken, misshapen and disharmonious, in direct reflection of the purity of the water source or its exposure to other elements. He exposed the water also to words or phrases such as "Thank you", "Love and Gratitude", "Worry", "Anxiety" and so on.

The results were amazing. Negative concepts produced water crystals which reflected the disharmony. The water labelled with loftier concepts and words produced beautiful snowflake-like patterns which in some ways related to the concepts expressed. Water exposed to the words: "I hate you and I want to kill you" actually formed into a shape that resembled a man holding a rifle.

The extrapolation that comes from this work and that should

most affect our thinking is when we realize that our bodies are 70% or more constituted by water molecules. The thoughts, feelings and tones we hold within us or we expose ourselves to, are creating harmony or otherwise in our physical make-up. It is happening right now ... right there in your body. Is it any wonder that for centuries meditation and serenity have been recommended for our wellbeing?

The extract quoted below is a paraphrased section from an interesting, but technically-worded document entitled "Philosophy" by unknown authors known as "The Wing Makers". (You can read more about the curious background of the document on an internet site by the same name.) It sets out some principles which are of interest and value, for your consideration.

Where "Source" is referred to you may wish to read "God", or whatever your concept may be of the Source of all things, or Supreme Power. The document is premised on the idea that our Universe has intelligence and design and works according to certain natural laws. The "Sovereign Integral" referred to is that point within each of us that is most closely aligned to our source, or to God:

> *"There are three particular life principles that accelerate the transformational experience and help to align a person with the Sovereign Integral perspective. They are:*
>
> *1) Universe relationship through gratitude;*
> *2) Observance of Source in all things;*
> *3) Nurturance of life.*

Universal Intelligence responds to our perceptions and expressions. It creates our reality around us; in the same way a pool of water mirrors the images that overshadow it. It can't help but reflect back to you the state of who you are and how you feel, because those are the images you are casting.

Every one of us, at our innermost core, is a Sovereign Entity who can transform ourselves into a conscious instrument of Creation, but what do we choose to create?

Do we project an image of our Divine Connection upon the mirror, or do we project a lesser image that is a distortion of our true state of being?

We consciously design our self image through **appreciation** *of the supportive mirror that is the Universal Entity. This is the principle of 'Universe Relationship through Gratitude'.*

In other words, the Universal Entity is a partner in shaping reality's expression in one's life.

Reality is an internal process of creation that is utterly free of external controls and conditions if the individual projects a sovereign image upon the mirror of the Universal Entity.

There is then an interchange of supportive energy from the Individual to the Universal Entity, and this energy is best applied through an appreciation of how perfectly and exactingly the mirror works at every moment.

If we are aware (or at least, interested in being aware), of how perfectly the Universe supports the reality we create, then there is a powerful and natural sense of gratitude that flows. It is this wellspring of gratitude that opens the channel of support from the Universe to the Individual, and establishes a collaboration to transform the Human into an expression of Source.

Time is the only factor that distorts this otherwise clear connection between the individual and Universal Entity. Time intervenes and creates pockets of despair, hopelessness, and abandonment.

However, it is these very 'pockets' that often activate our Source Codes and establish a more intimate and harmonious relationship with the Universal Entity.

Time establishes separation of experience and this creates doubt in the Universal Entity, its system of fairness and overarching purpose. In turn, this creates fear that the universe is not a mirror but rather a chaotic, whimsical energy.

When we are aligned with Source through gratitude and we live from this perspective, it attracts a natural state of harmony. That's not to say we don't have problems or discomforts, but when we do, we see these for what they are, that there is a purpose in what life reveals.

In order to create lasting joy and inner peace, our personal reality needs to flow from this perspective and this level of understanding.

Life mirrors back to us our intentions and when we appreciate this, we flow with this creation and appreciate and smile at how well it works."

SYNCHRONICITIES, INTUITION & COINCIDENCES

Do YOU HAVE those days when you just think of someone and then they phone or call in? ... Or when you have a feeling about something that turns out to be spot-on? It is not uncommon to hear of our sixth sense, and perhaps most of us have allowed that concept to be accepted in our view of the world these days.

As I write these words, I have just returned from visiting a friend and neighbour who asked if I had heard from another mutual friend of ours. I said I had not, but had just been thinking of her this morning. On my return from my visit, I was told that this mutual friend had just phoned and was on her way to visit me shortly. It will be the first time I have seen her in eight years!

As people have energy fields, their energy and intention travels out (like ripples in a pond) in front of them ... she has just arrived as I write these words, now.

Coincidentally, she is wearing a particular type of earring that I associate with her and which I was talking to someone about last night. She has also just been told by a friend before coming here that she should find and buy a particular book which I handed her shortly after she arrived ... (I have a shop) and she is reading it now, as I write this.

Do you see how waves of thought and intention echo out around us? And all of this just as I am writing this particular chapter!

There is a series of books by James Redfield – *The Celestine Prophecy, The Tenth Insight* and *The Secret of Shamballa,* each of which makes useful reading. While they are all written as fictitious stories, they depict things that are common to all of us and explain certain links and connections between us and how we live our lives. They are well worth reading, both as interesting stories and as a good basic education in the matters traversed.

One of the first things covered in the books is the relevance of coincidences and synchronicities, and the part they play in our lives. In your own life, make note of these things, because they are more often than not what I would call "echoes" of vibrations around us, or signs of what is manifesting in our lives.

As Redfield puts it: *" ...these coincidences are happening more and more frequently...They feel destined, as though our lives had been guided by some unexplained force. The experience induces a feeling of mystery and excitement and, as a result, we feel more alive. ...We are sensing ...that there is another side to life that we have yet to discover, some other process operating behind the scenes."*

Often important links and events that occur in life seemingly happen by pure chance or coincidence. Just think about how many times this is true in your own life: finding a job or a relationship; deciding on a new home or location: these are things we think we would plan carefully, but just as often they arise because of some twist of fate, like bumping into an old friend in the street, or finding an ad in a paper that blows by your door ...or something that would never have happened, had you turned left instead of right that day...

Just on that point, you may have seen this forwarded email (author unknown) that did the rounds some time after the 9/11 tragedy. It is a good illustration of the concepts above ...

> *"Just want to share a nice virtue. Don't be in a hurry, wait for His time. Next time your morning seems to be going wrong and the children are slow getting dressed and you can't seem to find the car keys and you hit every traffic light, don't get mad or frustrated; praise God instead because God is at work watching over you.*
>
> *After September 11, I happened to call for business a man that I didn't know and have not, nor will ever, talk to again. But this day, he felt like talking. He was head of security of a company that had invited the remaining members of a company who had been decimated by the attack on the Twin Towers to share their office space.*
>
> *With his voice full of awe he told me stories of why these people were alive and their counterparts were dead... and all the stories were just 'little' things.*
>
> *As you might know, the head of the company got in*

late that day because his son started kindergarten.

Another fellow was alive because it was his turn to bring donuts.

One woman was late because her alarm clock didn't go off in time.

One was late because of being stuck on the NJ Turnpike because of an auto accident.

One missed his bus.

One spilled food on her clothes and had to take time to change.

One's car wouldn't start.

One went back to answer the telephone.

One had a child that dawdled and didn't get ready as soon as he should have.

One couldn't get a taxi. There were other stories that I hope and pray will someday be gathered and put in a book.

The one that struck me was the man who put on a new pair of shoes that morning, took the various means to get to work but before he got there, he developed a blister on his foot. He stopped at a drugstore to buy a Band-Aid. That is why he is alive today.

Now when I am stuck in traffic, miss an elevator, turn back to answer a ringing telephone ... all the little things that annoy me ... I think to myself, this is exactly where God wants me to be at this very moment. May God continue to bless you with those annoying little things. May you remember their possible purpose."

FAIRIES, GHOSTS & OTHER WEIRD & OOKY-SPOOKY THINGS

COME ON NOW ... be truthful. Some of you will have seen something in your years of living, something you couldn't explain or rationalize away; whether it was a blur of light, a dark figure walking through a room, a deceased relative standing at the foot of your bed, orbs of light, fairies at the bottom of the garden, electric lights, phones, or devices turning themselves on or off for no reason, a feeling of paralysis while lying in bed half awake, or some other unexplained phenomenon.

These are more common than we realize, but most of the time people don't want to speak of these things or share their experiences for fear of being labelled a "Loony Tune". Alternatively, we forget these anomalies after a short time, for want of a rational pigeonhole to file them in.

These sightings and experiences could be any of a range of things... and are usually NOT weather balloons!

If we go back for a moment to the idea of dimensions, you will recall that while we live in our safe and rational third dimension, there are larger or different planes of existence outside of our own.

Life as we know it "vibrates" at a certain frequency, or speed. The atoms moving in our bodies vibrate at a certain rate, creating the illusion of solidness; whereas they are actually (and scientifically) groups of protons and electrons circling neutrons through quite a majority of empty space between.

Think for a moment of an electric fan ... When switched off, the blades are solid and you cannot see through them, but start the motor up and they spin. Then the blades appear to "disappear" in favour of a transparent motion blur.

Higher frequencies are similar. They do not appear "solid" unless they slow down to our frequency, or we speed up to theirs. We vibrate at our rate; other dimensions vibrate at higher or lower rates and exist at a different frequency, but can occupy the same *space* that we are in.

In this way, you might understand that if ghosts, fairies, space beings or Angels were to exist (just for the sake of the argument) they might not easily be perceived by us with our normal vision or senses.

Ask your dog if he is only *imagining* hearing a dog whistle. Just because *you* cannot hear it, does that mean it is not really whistling?

Sounds and colours exist on higher and lower frequency levels than our human senses can perceive. Our human instrument lives only within a certain range and can usually only pick things up within that range.

Psychics, Clairvoyants, Clairaudients, Mediums and Seers are just normal people who, for whatever reason, are attuned to a slightly different frequency than most of us, or who can raise or lower their vibration to perceive outside of the normal range of the majority.

It seems awfully unfair and unreasonable that these people are treated poorly by some, and outright disbelieved by others, just because their special talents are outside others' range of experience. The number of murders and other crimes that could be solved if police were willing to look at such information is great. The Australian/New Zealand television series *Sensing Murder* and others like it show excellent examples of fine work by psychics in this field.

Stories of Ghosts, Fairies, Angels, UFOs and other strange phenomena have lived on down the ages and there always are, always have been, and always will be people who see such things. Surely we are not willing to throw out centuries of observation and experience, just because we think it's all a little unlikely or we haven't seen it ourselves.

Before you rule out such phenomena, you should check to see if it is just fear of the unknown that is closing your mind to wider possibilities and fantastic worlds beyond your imagination. Fear can be overcome through understanding and a bit of healthy understanding might save a good percentage of our population from needless slurs upon their sanity in future.

As to the Beings that people do perceive, there seems to be life and a form of consciousness in a whole range of creations.

Fairies, for instance, are said to be the spirits of nature – those responsible for looking after the waters, earth, rocks, plants, trees, small animals and so on. They are overseen by larger entities or "Devas" who supervise a larger area, for instance a lake, a forest or a stream. There are any number of different such nature spirits whose appearance is reflective of that which they tend. Then there are certain Angelic Beings who overarch these domains at a higher level still.

Ranging up the scale to human life, we each come into this world with our own guardians and guides who are there to inspire and assist us should we ask. They also protect us from dangers we are not meant to experience.

Some know these as Guardian Angels and Spirit Guides. Again, there are countless stories of peoples' encounters with such Beings, often in life-saving situations. For reading on this subject there are many books on the market. Some that are worth mentioning here are: *Angel Visions I & II* by Doreen Virtue – two compilations of ordinary peoples' experiences and encounters with Angels or protective forces; and several books by Sylvia Browne, a down-to-earth American Medium, who has written extensively of her own experiences and connections with her Spirit Guide and teachers, including a book called *Life on the Other Side* which is a comfortable read about what one might expect to experience after death.

Fairies and Angels are different and separate from the ghosts or spirits of the deceased.

"Ghosts" are the disembodied consciousnesses of people who have departed. Often, if a death has been sudden or traumatic, a ghost might not realize they have "passed on" and will continue trying to go about life in the usual way, causing the living who perceive their presence to feel the place is haunted.

It is also the case that many people have *no belief* in an

afterlife. When they pass over, they find themselves confused because their consciousness is still living on, notwithstanding their belief that it would not. Until they learn and accept what is happening, these beings might surmise they are still alive and try to go about life as usual, sometimes causing ghostly sightings and occurrences. Commonly, these beings are encouraged to "move towards the light" to be helped by Angels and deceased loved ones to realize where they are and find peace in their new surroundings.

There are also descriptions of battlefields and other places of mass tragedy, where the high level of negative energy has created eerie feelings and ghostly sightings, almost like a "tape recording" of the disturbing energies and negativity on the land or area itself. This is apparently more likely to occur around bodies of water or in damp conditions, the water element being one which holds energies more readily.

In a slightly less "scary" category are encounters by people with a loved one who has departed, but made an appearance to express love, or a message or to say goodbye. Again, there are countless accounts of these experiences by ordinary folk, many of whom preface their story with words like "I don't believe in ghosts, but …"

One of the interesting physical signs of an extra-dimensional presence is that the temperature of the air tends to drop. People describe feeling the "hackles on their neck" standing on end and while fear or apprehension of the unknown is often present, the cold air temperature by itself largely contributes to this feeling. This has more to do with the difference in the vibration rate than it has to do with sensing "lurking evil". Remember, like in the movie *The Sixth Sense*, that just because an apparition may seem spooky or grotesque, it may well just be someone trying to get across some piece of important or relevant information from the Other Side. We should not automatically fear such things hysterically, but should try to keep an open mind and when in doubt, consult an appropriate expert on the subject.

Reputable mediums describe how our deceased loved ones can watch over us and relay information to help or warn us in our lives. The departed might communicate through a third party, such as a medium, or may make their presence felt more directly, if a person is open and attuned to picking up signs of their presence. People sometimes feel, for instance, like someone is tapping them lightly on the shoulder or foot when they are half asleep. This can be dear old grandma coming to say hello, so don't freak out automatically if you can avoid it!

It never ceases to amaze me how skeptics will discount as frauds people like Doris Stokes, John Edwards, or the like, just because imitators can show how the work of these mediums can be "mocked up" using some skilled guesswork and a large team of investigators. (I could use a calculator to find the answer to a math problem, but that doesn't prove that others could not do the same equation in their head!) It is undeniable that a person of fraudulent intent could indeed make a fair show of pretending such things, and natural caution on this note is not a bad thing, but that is not to say that there is no one in the world who IS the genuine article.

It is often just too convenient for a skeptic to write off *all* such practices as hoaxes, rather than looking more closely and deeply at their own beliefs and closed mind-sets and considering the facts openly. A questioning mind is a fair thing, as long as it is open to both sides of the argument and most skeptics' are not.

On the topic of people from outer space, even before Eric Von Daniken wrote *Chariots of the Gods* there has always been debate over whether we should believe in extraterrestrial life. Let me ask, what makes a person think that in the vastness of our Universe and its many dimensions, we are the only form of life that exists? Is this not a slightly over-inflated view of our uniqueness and importance in the grand scheme of things? The topic of extraterrestrials is a whole can of worms in itself – one that I think I'll return to in a later part of this book. For now, let's just let the idea of extra-dimensional life forms in general filter through your rational and intuitive senses and see how that settles.

Perhaps you'd like to enjoy a nice cup of tea, some jam and scones, and *lashings of ginger beer* before we approach *those mysteries*!

ASTRAL TRAVEL

To one side of our discussion of ghost and spirit energies, let me add another category of interdimensional visitor – the astral traveller. (And no, it's not *"Astro travel"* as many seem to call it.) You may well have heard of the notion – a person's astral or energy body floating up and out of the physical body during sleep, unconsciousness or deep relaxation. The astral body appears as an energy "replica" of the person's inert physical body and is attached to the physical body by what many have described as a Silver Cord of energy. When the astral body leaves the physical body it is able to move at will and with no space/time restrictions.

There are those who seem naturally to be able to achieve and remember conscious astral travel, there are those of us who feel the motion of flight in our dreams, but remember only the dream state, there are those who dearly would love to achieve such a thing ...

One man I met in my meditation group, Jamie, told us about his (then) recent and sudden initiation into astral travel. He described how he had for years had an annoying ringing in his ears (or like crickets) which as much as he tried to ignore, would bother him. When trying to sleep, he would have to work hard to shut out the sounds in his ears. One night, he said, he decided to listen to the sounds intensely and focus on them completely, as a new means of dealing with them. He did so and while focusing, it seemed the sounds carried him instantly into a state of astral projection. He found himself outside his body able to move around at will. The mere thought of where he would like to go would instantly bring him to that place. He found also that the feelings and emotions that accompanied this state of projection were of all-encompassing love and an awareness of the connection of all things and people to each other. He said that he would encounter others who were also projected out of their bodies and that they were visible to each other, but not necessarily to those in the waking reality.

There are, however, occasions when a person has seen the astral projection of someone they know and then verified the sighting with them afterwards. So, when you think you are seeing a ghost, or a spirit guide, you might actually be seeing the astral projection of someone "sleepwalking" through your space, or visiting you on purpose.

There is a book by Sylvan Muldoon and Hereward Carrington – *The Projection of the Astral Body* – which explores the whole astral travel area very well. It gives detailed information and instructions on how to achieve a state of consciously astral travelling if you desire.

Those who have experienced this phenomenon consciously, describe a peaceful and positive emotional state that goes with the experience: a reminder of their infinite nature.

One thing that can be disconcerting is the feeling of "falling" back into the body too quickly if a person is "out of body" and is woken suddenly. Also, if fear arises while the astral body is "out", it snaps back into the body sometimes causing a feeling of dizziness or disorientation for a moment or two. For a smoother ride, those learning to astral travel are encouraged to relax and flow with the experience, rather than tense up fearfully.

ORBS

Here's a strange thing I didn't know about until recently. I was out on the back deck once looking at distant lightning in some clouds and thought it might make an interesting photo, so I got the digital camera and tried to time my snaps to the lightning. The camera has a mind of its own and has to wait for the flash to charge up, whereas the term "Lightning fast" wasn't coined for nothing! In short I failed to capture the lightning itself, but just got shots of cloud ... or so I thought! On closer observation I noticed some small white "dots" in the clouds, which, when enlarged, appeared anomalous.

If you look on page 45 you'll find that first photo, followed by an enlargement. You can see for yourself the numerous dots ... (maybe with a magnifying glass!) This had me a little perplexed, so on subsequent evenings I went out with my husband, Briean and took more photos of the sky and then lowered the camera to take in neighbouring roofs and the back deck as well. What emerged was a series of shots with what we now know of as "orbs" appearing in multiples in the photos. In the colour section are some of the many shots and enlargements which illustrate this strange phenomenon ...

We now have hundreds of such photos, including ones taken indoors. We have shot at different locations and had friends use their own cameras with similar results. We have discovered there are a number of websites which feature exactly the same phenomenon all over the world, with the orbs showing up in fires and under water as well. (Search the Internet under the topic "Orbs" to see for yourself!)

Now *of course* we asked ourselves whether these are the result of light reflections, dust on the lens, and any number of different rational explanations ... and the people on the websites have also asked these things of their own shots, but no explanation seems to cover *all* of the circumstances in which the shots have been taken. The "dots" or "orbs" all bear a striking similarity to each other, no matter where in the world they are taken.

My own personal theory is that they are some sort of natural devic forces or extra dimensional presences in our midst. They seem more prevalent on overcast or rainy days, but look quite different from raindrops. We have also photographed airplanes and street lights to rule them out and they look nothing like these orbs.

The short point is: get your digital camera and go out a few times and take some shots yourself. It is only by seeing these with your own eyes, on your own camera, that you might start to realize how they are weirdly present, even in your own backyard.

We found that they seem to possess some sort of intelligence or consciousness of their own, because when we would "call them in" as if to take a group photo and count down from five to one before taking the shot, almost inevitably a large prominent one and many others would gather to be in the shot. You may like to try this yourself and see how you go. Make your own observations! Be your own detective. My guess is you'll find it enthralling. (Hint: when viewing on your computer, try boosting up the gamma level on darker pictures to reveal these orbs more clearly.)

As an interesting aside, we recently were with a real estate agent, viewing a property for sale, and took various shots of the house and yard for reference. Again, the orbs appeared.

There and then, we showed the photos to the agent, and keen to try for herself, she took some photos of her own. While she didn't capture any that day, she emailed the next day with some photos she took when originally listing the property months before ... complete with her own captured orbs! Have a go yourself and see what you think!

Another observation about these photos ... There was a second type of object that has shown up in some of them, which also remains unexplained: a "blue dot". In some of the shots of the sky and some taken indoors, there is a tiny but dense cobalt blue dot appearing. In one photo we have an airplane, two orbs and a blue dot all together in one frame.

The "blue dots" are so small they don't reproduce well, but a blown-up version appears here. When enlarged, they appear to have a white core, surrounded by the cobalt blue colour.

We profess no scientific or photographic expertise, so you

Helen M. Downs

may have a totally logical explanation for all of this, but as I have said, try a bit of your own photography and draw your own conclusions.

The photo was taken between lightning flashes on a stormy night. Note the numerous small white dots among the clouds.

An enlargement of one of the white dots.

These photos were taken the next night, one after the other. Orbs enlarged in insets.

In this shot, you can see orbs under the awning and outside in the open.

Right: One of the photos taken when visiting a property with the real estate agent.

Magic Eye® – Candy
(*See* p.9 for viewing instructions.)

Magic Eye® – Butterflies
(*See* p.9 for viewing instructions.)

Enlargement of the blue cobalt dot that also appears in some photos both indoors and outside.

Some photos and enlargements of other orbs captured on camera.

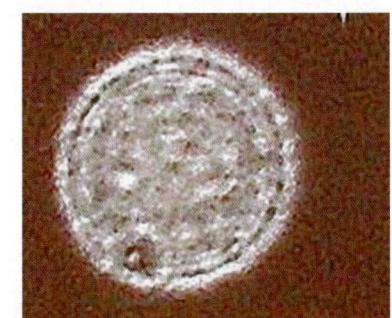

BODY, MIND, EMOTIONS ...

WE OFTEN TALK about these three areas as if they operate independently of each other, and to a certain extent they do. But much research has been done, looking at the links. You may be surprised to learn that ill-health and disease are the ***direct out-workings of our mental and emotional states.***

Popular "New Age" author, Louise Hay, wrote a book back in the 1980s, called *You Can Heal Your Life,* in which she talks about her own battle with cancer and how she not only overcame it, but realized the connection between emotions, beliefs, thoughts and our health. The book alphabetically lists dozens of physical conditions and beside them, lists the thought pattern or belief that creates the particular condition. It's worth taking a look because such a list gives you the opportunity to translate what your body is trying to tell you about your state of consciousness.

At first you may laugh at the concept and say that susceptibility to disease and accidents is merely bad luck and cannot possibly be created by a person. Who would want to break their leg? Or contract Cancer? Preposterous!! Yet the more you look into this, the more you see it is true. (Not that people consciously *choose* these misfortunes, but that we *attract* them by holding a state of mind or belief over time.)

Returning to the idea of vibrations and how we create the reality around us, we can see how our body is one of the first places where those vibrations will manifest.

For a person who finds it hard to speak up for themselves, for instance, the problem is likely to manifest in the throat, by way of a tickle, a cough, congestion or something more developed. People who are "one eyed" in their views might find their vision impaired or affected; those intolerant or not open to hearing points of view other than their own may have a diminution in the functions of their ears.

The list compiled by Hay goes into more detail on many complaints and suggests for each, a healing attitude and affirmation to rectify the condition. Her work was further developed by Annette Noontil in *The Body is the Barometer of the Soul II*. These books are highly recommended as helpful day to day references and tools. Noontil lists individual bones, teeth, vertebrae and organs, and tells how their functions relate to a particular thought pattern or issue that we may be blocked on. She even has a secondary list of car "ailments" and what these tell you about your direction in life; for example, a flat battery indicates a need to rejuvenate yourself with new plans, while problems with the fan belt relate to a need to understand yourself better in order to power your progress.

Don't just write off these correlations because you do not think the link is possible. Remember, if you could see it from a wider viewpoint, it would make a lot of sense, and there are those who *can* encompass this wider view comfortably. Knowledge is power, and to investigate and understand these connections and keep yourself in good health puts you in a far stronger position! Know Yourself!

This leads us tangentially to another aspect of health and emotion. Where does a pain, hurt or trauma go when we do not express, acknowledge or release it? Answer: it is stored in the body in some way and we tend to hide, protect and cover it with other patterns of behaviour to avoid being hurt again in a similar way. Like an injured ankle when we favour it over time by walking a different way, we build up self-protective behaviours which affect other parts of our system...both muscles and attitudes...eventually leading to other imbalances.

This is why it is helpful to find ways of releasing stored fears, hurts, anger and such emotions that are otherwise held, maybe for a lifetime, to our potential detriment.

There are a number of different methods and therapies for such release, or for general wellbeing. Below is a list (certainly not exhaustive!) of modalities that are at your disposal for helpful treatments or practices:

Acupuncture, Alexander Technique, Aromatherapy, Ayurvedic Medicine, Bowen Therapy, Chinese Herbal Medicine, Crystal Therapy, Clinical, Remedial & Hawaiian style Massage, Counselling, Dance/Movement Therapy, Feldenkreis, Flower Essence Therapy, Homeopathy, Horstmann Technique, Hypnotherapy,

Iridology, Kinesiology, Naturopathy, Neuro Linguistic Programming, Pilates, Pranic Healing, Qi Gong, Rebirthing, Reconnective Healing, Reflexology, Reiki, Shiatsu, Spiritual Healing, Tai Chi, Trigger Point Therapy, Thought Field Therapy, Touch for Health, Yoga ... the list goes on!

Of the above I will make specific mention of a few modalities which are easily accessible in most places and can spearhead immediate shifts and improvements in one's life.

Kinesiology uses a method called "muscle testing" to elicit answers from the body directly, without the patient having to rely solely on what they are consciously thinking.

You know yourself there are many who are in denial of their true emotions or feelings and may answer "no" to a question where deep down (and perhaps unbeknownst to them) the answer is "yes". Through muscle testing (testing strength or weakness from moment to moment in answer to different questions) the practitioner can get to the core of issues that hold back success, health and wellbeing.

There are various developed methods based on Kinesiology, including Kinergetics, Touch for Health, R.A.W. and Three in One Concepts' One Brain System. These have intricate methods of retrieving and working with information kinesthetically, to heal or resolve stresses and blockages. For an example, you may not be aware of something that your mother or father said to you when you were three years old, but which had adversely affected your behaviours or belief in yourself ever since then.

The practitioner would locate such causes and neutralise their effect, giving you back freedom to make new conscious choices in response to similar stimuli in future. The analogy often used is that our consciousness is like an iceberg, with a small percentage above the waterline (what we know we are thinking or feeling) but a much larger portion below the water (what we are unaware is motivating our behaviours and choices). These therapies will effectively locate and deal with the hidden aspects that steer our responses to life's stimuli.

"Thought Field Therapy" (or TFT) is another very effective technique which combines tools from Kinesiology, Acupressure and Neuro Linguistic Programming, to quickly and painlessly remove the effects of fears, trauma, anxieties and so on. American Psychotherapist, Dr. Roger Callahan, developed this modality, in which sequences of meridian points are tapped with two fingers to bring immediate and lasting (some would say miraculous!) solutions to problems ranging from passing sadness to post traumatic stress disorders.

This method has been described as being like bringing up a computer programme file (from the brain) and hitting the delete key. People with phobias such as, for example, a fear of snakes, have been demonstrated to lose such a fear within minutes, using this method. Courses in Thought Field Therapy are available and can be completed over a weekend for a very reasonable price. If you have the opportunity to attend, it is well worth the investment. Alternatively, description of the method can be found in Dr. Callahan's book: *Tapping the Healer Within.*

Reiki is a popularly recognized energy healing modality with effects that range from relief from pain to total healing of physical and emotional conditions, using the laying on of hands by a practitioner who has been attuned to these energies. It is perhaps one of the better known therapies and you can usually find a Reiki practitioner close by, wherever you live.

Dr. Eric Pearl has written a book called *The Reconnection* which speaks of his experiences in discovering this amazing energy modality (Reconnective Healing). The book is self-explanatory and is well worth reading for insights into his most interesting true story and his work in this field.

There are also a number of other energy therapies, based in many traditional and newly uncovered sources. The important basic rule of thumb is that such therapies should be aimed at empowering you, not making you dependant upon the practitioner. In these types of healing modalities the underlying factor is the notion that each person needs to take responsibility for their wellbeing, rather than thinking or feeling it is someone else's task to make them better. Remember: you are creating your life and your reality!

In all cases, where a physical "shift" or cure takes place, it is necessary that the emotional or mental attitude which created the condition in the first place, be also resolved or released. Otherwise, the condition is likely to recur, or reassert itself in another way.

There are any number of stresses, anxieties and conditions that medical science and psychotherapy are unsuccessful in treating, except through (potentially harmful) pharmaceuticals or surgery, but which can be effectively addressed using alternative methods such as those listed and described above. While medical advice should always be sought, don't limit your options to just the conventional approaches they encourage.

Through my meditation group, I have had the good fortune to have met a French lady named Josette Simon. Formerly a top pattern cutter in Milan and Turin, for Versace and other big name design houses, she went on to study *Human and Universal Energy Healing* in Geneva, Switzerland, at first only pursuing it to (successfully) heal her much-loved dog from the after-effects of cancer treatment. Now, years later, Josette regularly treats a variety of people and animals using energy. She stresses regularly (in her characteristic French accent) the benefits of a healthy diet in maintaining good health and recommends fresh organic fruit and vegetables, fresh juices and lots of water. This kind of diet is almost impossible for a lot of us to conceive or realize, but even for a short time (three days or three weeks) it is certainly worth a try for a good cleansing of the system. Josette's personal energy is always high and her abilities speak for themselves. Within her own body she feels the patient's pains and imbalances and directs energy to rectifying these imbalances. Rather than seeing illness as a diagnosed or terminal condition, she sees the energy blocks or deficiencies that create the condition and treats these directly to restore wellbeing. I and others I know have witnessed first-hand her healing abilities and have felt immediate lightness and physical upliftment after a short session with her. She can diagnose and treat over the phone as easily as in person and her skills and gifts are indeed a blessing to all who have benefited.

There are people like this in most communities these days. They are worth finding and consulting if you have health problems that conventional medicine does not satisfactorily address. It serves you to investigate these therapies and try them for yourself.

A common objection is: 'Oh that's all nice but it won't work for *me*!' or 'Yes, but you don't understand how serious/

unsolvable/long-term *my* condition is!' Everyone seems to have what they think is a good reason why it can't or won't work, without even giving it a go. Before you reject or ignore such therapists, ask yourself if you are willing to rule out the potential for wellness and emotional balance just because of some fear or a lack of understanding?

There are also people who have a lot invested in their state of poor health. It serves to get them sympathy, attention, or give them power where they otherwise would have to focus on getting on with life. In such cases, the person may not want to get well, and will undermine or sabotage their own healing process.

If you object to alternate therapies as a solution to your own unsolvable case, ask yourself what stops you wanting to improve or believing you can. This may well be part of what needs healing and should not be disregarded. In cases of religious objections, Jesus Himself exhibited these healing abilities and stated that all of these things *you can do too!* So what's stopping you from trying?

MEDITATION, YOGA, TAI CHI & THE LIKE ...

So what's the go with these practices? And why do people do them?

The thing these have in common is that they allow a person to still the mind and in the case of Yoga and Tai Chi, the body is also gently exercised in certain ways that induce a more harmonious state.

These ancient practices were developed using knowledge of the requirements of the body's energy system and the meridians and chakras we have spoken of previously. While running and swimming will provide good exercise, these ancient practices use each movement and breath to enhance or build the energy, in keeping with the natural flows within our bodies.

I am not usually one for exercise myself and generally have to be dragged kicking and screaming (well, almost) to go for a walk. Some years ago, I tried to stimulate some interest in my body's wellbeing by attending classes in Qi Gong (meaning "energy work") and Tai Chi, held by a Chinese Master. I can say from these experiences, that such exercises *can and do* help not only physically, but also they raise one's vibration, mental clarity and awareness.

On one occasion the Master worked directly on my energy flow. That night at home, my body had the urge to move around to get the circulation going, quite independently of my conscious mind, which would have remained on the couch if it had its way. My legs were marching on the spot and my arms waving around in circles and it felt uncomfortable to just sit down, until the movements abated.

I found this curious and non-threatening and interesting proof of how people skilled in these areas can have a positive effect on the overall system of wellness. It is, of course, up to us to continue with such practices or sink back into complacency… but such Masters can certainly provide a good kick-start to the system.

Exercises such as Tai Chi and Yoga have a strong component of breathing within them. Breathing is an important part of all such practices, because it is our way of linking ourselves directly with how we are feeling and what we are perceiving … contacting our own Spirit.

The depth and calmness with which we breathe feed into our overall wellbeing and are perhaps the simplest things we can do to restore balance for ourselves. In stressful moments it is always advisable to pause for a few moments to take at least three deep breaths before continuing. This helps to centre you and brings more calm to you and therefore, the situation.

You may have heard of a practice called "Rebirthing". This is based on using the breath to access emotions which have been locked inside our bodies, possibly as long ago as at the time of birth.

As they explain, have you noticed when something shocking or awful happens, the first thing we do is take a sharp breath in and hold it – often putting our hand over our mouth as well? Apparently this action serves to "shield" us from what we are experiencing or witnessing, but also traps our feelings in the body. The appropriate way to remain clear and prevent these emotions being held to our detriment is to ensure we continue breathing deeply through any such upsetting occurrence.

The practice of rebirthing takes you through extended breathing exercises to bring up and let go of pains, traumas and fears that can otherwise remain trapped in the body, or psyche, creating actions or reactions based on past experiences, rather than the current facts.

Practices like Yoga and Tai Chi are also ways of moving stuck energy through the physical body. Those who developed these exercises were familiar with the channels of energy and how they can be mobilized to bring smooth flow and clarity into one's body and life.

Meditation is something you can do in a group or in isolation. In short, it gives you a mental space to become more aware of your true essence and to connect with the guidance that comes to you from what may be called your "Higher Self".

Some have said that prayer is when we ask God a question and meditation is when we listen for an answer. In a state of meditation, you are able to tune also to your body (or the world at large) and feel what messages may be conveyed to you.

For example, an ache or a pain is not just a random thing. It is your body sending a signal that something needs attention. By quietly placing your focus on the area, thoughts may arise as to appropriate steps to take to remedy or relieve the strain.

Most people find it difficult to sit still and empty their mind or focus on one thing for any length of time and may become impatient, but if they persist beyond this point they will find the benefits to be ... well ... beneficial!

Methods of meditation can be as simple as focusing on only one thing, such as one's breathing, or a candle flame. There are also guided meditations, where you are given instruction on colours or images to picture in your mind as you breathe in a relaxed manner. Some require only that you repeat to yourself a "mantra" or words that induce a deeper state of relaxation or connectivity.

As mentioned in an earlier chapter, the chakras can be visualized and "cleared" by mentally picturing them so. Also by focusing, for instance, on bringing healing to one's body or to another person, these effects can also be achieved. In short, whatever you choose to focus on and direct your energy towards can be amplified by achieving a deep, calm state of mind while doing so.

People who practise energy-healing therapies in person, usually can also "send" such healing from a distance, while in a meditative state.

An interesting story about one such person is found in the book: *Conversations with the Body* by Robyn Elizabeth Welch, who carries out healings by using a disciplined mental focus, without having to touch the patient's body, or even view the person with her physical sight. She has cleared away many tumours and seemingly incurable conditions with success.

Very often healers, like Robyn Welch, have gone through years of struggle and have had to deal with healing crises in their own lives before becoming masters in their field. The practice of meditation in one form or another has usually been part of the backdrop in their self-education to reach this point of accomplishment and it has usually been something that has developed slowly over time, in between living a "normal" day to day life in the "real world".

You may be a person who has a bit of a sixth sense or a knack for calming animals, children or others. Who knows? You may have hidden or dormant talents and gifts that are yet to be developed in the years to come. A good starting point inevitably is to begin to clear away blocks to your own development and positive creativity.

The modalities described above and in the previous chapter provide ways to do this – coupled with a genuine interest in your spiritual side and its development. Balanced growth as a self-aware person, creating a positive reality for yourself and others in your life can be achieved. The starting point is in your mind, thoughts and an open attitude!

PALMISTRY, ASTROLOGY, NUMEROLOGY & TAROT

MOST PEOPLE HAVE at one time or another had their palms or cards read, had someone figure out their birth numbers, or looked at their astrology predictions.

As a rule, the more general the reading (i.e. that you get in the daily newspapers) the less specific and accurate it is likely to be. Many factors need to be taken into account for proper readings to be compiled and these modalities should not be judged badly, based on light generalities.

The basic idea behind all such sciences (and they *are* sciences in their own ways) is that all things have their own resonance and depending on the conditions surrounding you, certain of these resonances will have their effect on your personality, your future, or your responses to things.

In the case of astrology, the position of the planets at your time of birth provides a "stamp" of energy that is unique to that moment and can be analyzed and explained by a trained practitioner. One of the best authors to describe the nature of each Sun sign is Linda Goodman, who wrote many books in her time. Her best-known is *Sun Signs* and gives you a beautifully-written rundown on the general personality traits you can expect to find in each sign.

More recently, the work of Jan Spiller in *Spiritual Astrology* and *Astrology for the Soul* (amongst others) provides uncanny insights into the inclinations arising from individual planetary positions.

The numerical value of your name or date of birth has a resonance that emanates from your energy field. In Numerology, the digits of the full date of birth are added together and then reduced to a single digit, to reveal truths about the personality. Similarly, the letters in one's name can be converted to numbers and reduced to one or more single digits with their own resonance. The classical works of Cheiro and other more recent authors can be accessed to know more on these topics.

Here is an interesting example of good effective use of numerology, contained in an episode of the TV series, *Sensing Murder*.

In the episode, an unsolved murder mystery was posed to a few top psychics for their input. One of them, well-known Australian psychic, Scott Russell-Hill, pointed to a vital clue which effectively unravelled the whole mystery. After calculating the numerology of the victim, he concluded that she could not have died on the date that was, until then, assumed to be the date of death. It was more likely she had died the day before, he said, because the preceding date was more consistent with important destiny codes in the victim's numerology.

When his theory was followed up and investigations were carried out at the location where the victim was known to be on the *preceding* day, her blood was indeed found at that location, on a newspaper dated the day *before* the death was thought to have occurred! As a result, a whole new line of investigation was considered, providing an answer to what otherwise may have remained a mystery. *(Fine work Scott!)* This example shows the practical and useful applications that a science such as numerology can be put to, if we are willing to keep an open mind.

In palmistry, it is said that the map of your life can be read from the lines on your hands. Again, the resonance that you hold is expressed in the lines on the hands and can change as you change. The shapes and lengths of the fingers and hands also play a part in defining the personality and experiences of their owner. Apparently, *my* palms say that I am likely to write books and become fabulously successful! (Publishers should ignore this information at their own risk!!)

Tarot or even plain playing cards when read, are perhaps slightly less scientific, but can also prove amazingly accurate. The illustrations on the original tarot decks are drawn from major archetypal experiences, coupled with the more mundane occurrences signified in the "suit" cards. A client's resonance is again the factor which causes the cards that are chosen to be relevant in the reading. The cards are interpreted by a skilled reader, using a combination of set meanings and some intuitive input as well.

In all types of reading, don't knock it until you have tried it! A good accurate reading from a professional will do more

A Handful of Seeds

to prove validity than thousands of words written by me. Countless books are available on these subjects for those who wish to study them further and every city has its fair share of skilled practitioners in these fields. Find a practitioner who is well recommended though, as with everything, there are always dodgy ones and it is unfair if a bad apple should spoil an otherwise good bunch!

While it is often the case that people want to know their future, they are perhaps better served to use such readings as a spiritual tool to assess "where they are at" in relation to their intended life path and their best development. The power of suggestion is indeed strong and too many people rely on what they are told rather than discerning for themselves what they choose to create in life. The tools of tarot and other readings are, in my opinion, best used to ascertain the terrain through which one is travelling, so as to know the "lie of the land" so to speak. In this way the client can feel more peace of mind when navigating life's twists and turns, while maintaining freedom to choose their own path and make their own decisions.

One should also be aware of the type of reader from whom they seek advice. While there are people with genuine gifts and talents in psychic fields, there are different levels or dimensions from which they draw their insights.

Those drawing from lower levels (sometimes known as the "astral" plane) can be more inclined to create worry, dread or dependency in their client, rather than genuinely assisting them along their life's path. Predictions of imminent death or disease for instance, are not generally helpful and serve only to upset and de-energize a client, whereas a timely warning to look after your health or diet, coupled with encouragement for more positive aspects to dwell upon can uplift and assist in far more positive ways. Generally, if you feel a reading is laced with negativity, apply your own good judgement, step out of that space and call in more positive energies to guide and protect you.

This advice doesn't just apply to psychic territories. Think about the car mechanics or builders who have inspected and quoted you on repair jobs. There are just as many people in *all sorts of fields* who will prey on your insecurities and create worry and dependency if you allow it. Readers have their own personalities, like everyone else and *some* are on an ego trip or in a negative space, in the way they deliver their information to you. If decent, caring and helpful sensitivity is not present, then nor should you be.

ANGELS, GUIDES & GUARDIANS

I N BIBLICAL TIMES, it seems everyone was being visited by an Angel who was announcing something. Artistic works from the time of Michelangelo and his contemporaries were full of Angelic imagery. These days, we'd find it rather odd to see a brilliant haloed and winged figure appearing in our lounge. (We'd probably ask him to keep quiet until the commercial break.) Yet, there are actually many people who have experienced Angelic presences in the course of their lives. Unfortunately, most people are hesitant to speak about these things, lest they be labelled a fruitcake.

It never ceases to amaze me that the churches, which promote stories of these great beings, are usually the first to denounce stories of personal encounters with Angels, as if they are real, but not *really* real – they happen in history, but not in the NOW.

As mentioned in an earlier chapter, there are books which set out dozens of personal accounts of appearances by Angelic beings in times of trouble or danger, or to bring comfort or a message.

If you read the opening pages of the book of Mormon, you will see the sworn testimonies of the four men who were present to see the appearance of the Angel Moroni to the Prophet Joseph Smith in the early 1800s. A further eight men testify to having seen the engraved plates delivered by this Angel.

In other writings, there are accounts of people watching TV when the screen has gone blank, and an Angel has appeared and delivered a message using this modern medium.

So who are they and what are they doing? We are told that at birth we are given at least two Guardian Angels who are there to watch over us for our entire life. American medium Sylvia Browne tells us that she has seen increasing numbers of Angels surrounding her clients in more recent times. She and many others describe how, before we embark upon our earthly lives, we are involved in the planning of our lifetime and the lessons we will come here to learn about and master. Our Angels and Spirit Guides are our helpers who watch over us from the Other Side to assist us on our path and who are always lovingly in attendance.

If these extra-dimensional Beings are there for all of us, to help us with life's flow, then why do so few of us take the whole thing seriously, or treat it as if it is real? It seems there has been an age old conspiracy to keep us in the dark and disconnect us from our spiritual roots and links to these other-worldly dimensions. Our modern lifestyles and technologies have perhaps drowned out the voice of our own inner knowings and promptings and cut us off from remembering why we are here in the first place.

If we were a little more open in considering these possibilities in our lives, we might see evidence that "synchronistic good" has been there all along, gently supporting us and urging us onward in times where we otherwise may have given up, or gone another way. Many books and writings show and tell us how we can make contact with our Angelic guidance and learn to work in co-operation with our Higher Purpose and direction in life.

We can start by making time to tune in, with the quiet of a still mind, and listen for our true inner urgings and messages. We *can* speak to God directly, or to our Angels, knowing that they will hear us, even if we do not feel we can hear their responses. We *can* ask for what we wish to create and achieve in our lives – *Ask and ye shall receive.* The first thing to do, though, is to stop and remember and consider this dimension in our lives, instead of dismissing it as the work of fiction and fantasy.

The difference between Spirit Guides and Angels, some say, is that an Angel is an extra-dimensional Being of a particular level, who was created as an Angel and not an incarnate Human Being. A Guide is a Spirit who *has been* incarnate, experienced human life and achieved levels of learning and wisdom sufficient to fill their role as a Guide. Both categories can assist us from their other-worldly place, although (not unlike in the Star Trek *Prime Directive*) they cannot interfere with our free choices. They can only intervene if their help is requested.

As described in a previous chapter, we also have deceased relatives and friends who sometimes fill roles as guides of sorts, in their efforts to watch over and protect us. Our Spirit

Guides, however, are the ones who remained on the Other Side from before our birth, with the job of looking after our development.

People have developed good working relationships with these Guides and Angels in their lives. Some who are particularly "tuned in" can hear, see or sense these extra-dimensional Beings and communicate meaningfully with them. They invariably report the relationship to be of great assistance, value and comfort in their lives. We too, can develop such a relationship by focusing on our desire to do so and working on it over a time.

Something I have found in this regard is that the guidance or information is best received when one is in the course of actively going about the work at hand. When theoretical questions are asked, or questions just for the sake of them, it seems harder to get an answer or an intuition on the subject, whereas when one genuinely needs help while engaged in some project or decision, the answer is more likely to "pop out of the air" in some way.

Briean describes how he found himself in a situation where, having never flown a plane before, an emergency arose requiring someone to land the light aircraft he was on. Having dreamed the night before that he was successfully flying, he volunteered to make the landing, notwithstanding his lack of actual experience in this regard. He said he was filled with a sense of certainty that he could do it, and as *someone* had to do *something*, he figured they had nothing to lose, as all was lost anyway if no one tried. He did indeed land the plane successfully and the lives of all on board were saved as a result! He doesn't know what made him think he could do it but, in the dire circumstances, he trusted the intuition that was telling him what to do, with great results.

While I am not suggesting that we all go out and fly planes tomorrow, without the ability, you can see in this example how when the information or know-how is needed, we can call it up and use it. This is what the connection with our Guides and Angels is all about – and we all have the ability to call upon it.

EXTRATERRESTRIALS – IS THERE LIFE OUT THERE?

THERE SEEMS TO be an international pastime that consists of mocking anyone who professes to have seen a UFO or had any dealings with people from out of this world. Funnily, as soon as someone mentions that they have perceived anything along these lines, even the open-minded among us seem to think there is something a little loopy going on and we shut down and become very narrow-minded quite suddenly.

The first thing people who have seen a UFO seem to do is resolve not to talk about it or tell anyone what they saw ... and quite rightly, it seems, as the treatment received by those who *do* tell, makes it hardly worth the effort. Disbelief, ridicule and worse, are the responses our society has been conditioned to dish out for these occasions.

To start at the other end of the equation though, we find that not only do such things exist, but that there are those on Earth who have been communicating with extraterrestrials and even visiting their ships with regularity. Those who have written extensively on the subject go as far as to list dozens of extraterrestrial races, their descriptions and something of their agendas in relation to our planet and our species.

When you think about it coolly and rationally, why in the world would there *NOT* be others sharing this vast universe with us? What would make us think we are the *only* possible form of life that exists in the infinite space that extends for millions of light years around us? From airline and air force pilots, astronauts and retired military officials, to police officers and the common man or woman in the street, thousands have come out and said that they have indeed witnessed events or activities that are out of this world. Some governments are so accomplished at denying such things that they actually set up official departments to maintain these denials. (A strange thing to do really, as you don't see official secret intelligence organizations formed to counter our beliefs about Santa Claus or the Tooth Fairy, so why is this done for UFOs if they are NOT real?)

I find it somewhat amusing that scientists send probes to Mars looking for water molecules or minute cells of possible amoebic life forms, to see if there is life "out there", while in Mexico people are photographing "flaps" (the name given to sightings of large numbers of ships in an area), with UFOs zipping around the sky in those unexplained manoeuvres, seen by literally hundreds of people at a time. When will rational science open its eyes to what is happening all around us? Any TV documentary on the subject spends an awful lot of time showing old black and white footage of Roswell and Area 51 stories, presumably in an effort to bore the viewer to death, before reaching a conclusion like: "*We may NEVER know what the truth is...blah blah blah*", yet there are so many who could tell so much, if there was a genuine interest by the public to know more.

Perhaps it is too far removed from our mundane day to day reality to contemplate these subjects, or it makes us too uncomfortable to think that our limited views of what is real should be challenged. It is thought that we are shielded by Governments from the reality of extraterrestrials so as to avoid mass panic, like that which occurred when Orson Welles took to the airwaves with his famous radio play *War of the Worlds*.

As a population, are we *ready* to handle the awesome truth? When we show a little maturity in this regard, perhaps we'll be fed more of the real story – that which we are certainly being deprived of "for our own good" and /or for other reasons at the moment.

On an individual level, it might be a step in the right direction to check ourselves next time we go to automatically bag a person who professes a faith in our space brethren, or is disturbed by something they saw but cannot believe, understand or explain. Referral to the nearest psych unit is not always the best solution!

In all those movies, you see the person who has witnessed ET activity becoming increasingly frustrated as their loved ones write them off as a bad joke, then pack up and go live with their mother. Would this be your response too? Ask yourself why your mind would be so closed to the potential reality of ETs in our midst. It usually boils down to fear of

A Handful of Seeds

the unknown, but sticking your head in the sand is hardly a viable solution.

There is also an amount of fear by many people who have actually experienced (or suspect they have experienced) abductions by ETs ... more people than you might think! Those who are able to recall such experiences report being medically examined or probed, under restraint, while on board a space ship and then returned to their home, usually in the dead of night. Others report the experience of missing time, where they have driven along a (usually remote) road, possibly seen strange lights in the sky and then eventually arrived at their destination twenty minutes or an hour later than the trip would have warranted.

Others have felt a strange sleep paralysis while in bed at night and have seen the characteristic odd figures of ETs standing around their bed. So what is happening? Are they all suffering some kind of mass delusion, borne of one too many Steven Spielberg movies? The rational-minded skeptics would have us believe this is so, and if it still comforts you to think so, you may choose to continue to side with them for the moment, but one day in the future, when a space ship lands in your backyard and little gray guys step onto your lawn, don't say I didn't try and apprise you of their existence!

For those who have some curiosity as to who they are and what they want, read on. For the others, you might like to hum a nice tune and close your eyes for a few more paragraphs ...

Writings and accounts on these subjects suggest that there are a number of different races of ET in our midst, each with its own agenda for being here. It all gets a little weird to hear about in depth, so I'll try and narrow it down to a few of the more relevant or commonly applicable parts, while bearing in mind that the ultimate truth of "what is out there" is so much *out of our present paradigm* that it would, no doubt, defy our understanding or grasp as yet.

Humans, as a race (or at least most of us) are said to have originated in the stars, rather than here on this planet. The Earth has, according to writings on this topic, been populated and colonized many times by different extraterrestrial races during different periods from ancient pre-history onwards. The civilizations of Atlantis and Lemuria are just two, perhaps better known, examples of lost races that lived on the Earth. Some studies of how the pyramids were built and their purpose, point towards technologies having been available in those times, including levitation devices, utilizing sound frequency technology to alter density of matter – technologies that point to the existence of highly advanced civilizations that have been here before us.

In our lives in the current here and now, we are said on the whole to have forgotten our origins and the vastness of the cosmic history we came from. Some people suspect that they are not actually "from here" but have no idea how true this feeling may really be.

Extraterrestrial races said to be interacting with our planet, even now, come from star systems including, but not limited to: Sirius, The Pleiades, Zeta Reticuli, Apollonia, Maldek (a destroyed moon that orbited Mars and is now an asteroid belt), Orion, Vega, Arcturius and Nibiru (a planet whose orbit allegedly comes within range of Earth only every 3,600 years, the last time being around 0 AD) … to mention just a few.

Natives of these other worlds are said to have their own reasons and agendas for being here, but it seems commonly accepted in a cross-section of works on these topics, that the Earth is unique and special due to its vibrational density and the evolutionary stage that we are entering at this time; thus there is much extraterrestrial interest in this planet right now. It is said that extraterrestrial races have been involved in an age-old struggle (along the classic good v evil lines) and that those with their own self interests at heart have been keeping our Earthly population subdued, creating war and havoc, while feeding on our emotions of fear and hatred, which they inspire and fuel for their own ends. Ultimately, the population of Earth is beseeched to "wake up" and realize the gross manipulation of our will that has been taking place. We are meant to start creating for ourselves, with the power of our thoughts and our will, an alternative, *better* world than that which has been created around us by those who have thus far had the power to do so.

Some of the extraterrestrial races are said to be monitoring our evolutionary progress and offering the wisdom of their knowledge and experience to humans with whom they have been in contact. There are many websites on the Net which you can look at to see examples of messages purportedly received from our space brethren.

Historically, there was a marked increase in UFO sightings from the 1940s when nuclear weaponry experiments commenced. Apparently, having gone through their own bad experiences in the past, some ETs are here to see that we do not bring about the extinction of our own species not only to our detriment, but also to that of those who share our universe, which would be adversely affected by nuclear weaponry.

Others appear to have an interest in our Spiritual development (interwoven as it is with our potential self-destruction).

There are many reports of persons taken on board ships and given instruction and teachings on matters of spirituality, human evolution and our existence so they may pass this knowledge on to others.

One of the most common races that we as humans seem to have been exposed to in media depictions is the "Gray" race – the space brethren hailing from the Zeta Reticuli constellation. These are the ones whose appearance is depicted in the Spielberg movies, and his series *Taken*. They are described as usually short (around the four foot mark) and of grayish or blueish skin colour. They have small openings at the mouth and long thin fingers and limbs. They communicate telepathically.

As they have the ability to travel both through space and time, we have apparently come into contact with ones from their race from past, present and future times, each with a different level of understanding or "politeness" towards our species. They are commonly thought of as having more of a scientific than compassionate approach towards us and are involved in programmes of interracial breeding, producing hybrid children from both our race and theirs. (The reason for this it seems, is that they somehow "bred out" their ability to feel emotions and need to reintroduce this component to their race for its future wellbeing.)

It is thought that in years gone by this race entered into some secret arrangement with high level government to allow the breeding programme to occur, and their existence is kept secret because of the poor response the public would rightly have to knowing about the whole deal.

On a Spiritual level, however, it is also asserted that *our own Spirits* agreed (unbeknownst, perhaps, to our conscious minds) to interact with these beings, before we came into our lives in this world. On this unconscious level, we (or at least those who did so agree), have given consent to be monitored and experimented upon, for the good of our mutual species, and/or to have our eggs or sperm used for interracial breeding purposes. While it all sounds very mechanical (and indeed this race is not known for their kindness or understanding of our needs and comforts), there are writings that suggest that these Beings actually assist the Angels, attend on the sick while they sleep, amongst other things, to bring healing, and that they also bring teachings and higher wisdoms to other members of our race. In this regard they are said to work in conjunction with Beings of certain other species as well.

An interesting (and perhaps uncharacteristically kind) account of our interactions with the Gray race can be found in the book *Looking Through Eyes of Love* by Judy Carroll, an Australian authoress. In the introduction, she describes her account as fictional (the story itself is a composite of experiences and not strictly factual in that regard) but she also intimates that there is more truth to the accounts generally than that of just a fairytale.

I have had the opportunity to meet and share an evening with this lady, who in her book writes of being a human incarnation of one of the Gray race, who regularly attends on board their ships at night to carry out the work which she is given to do. She explains that in vast Spiritual terms, we are all part of one big family and that her race is helping us with our Spiritual and Physical evolution.

After Judy attended and spoke with our meditation group one evening, one of the other participants, who happens to be clairvoyant herself, reported hearing movement in her house the next two nights, as she lay awake in bed. Surprisingly to herself, she did not get up to investigate (there being no one else in the house, which was all locked up) but as she lay there, she saw a number of the Gray figures gathered around her bed for long enough for her to ascertain she was not dreaming or hallucinating, before they slowly disappeared. Even she, who is accustomed to seeing Spirits and supernatural sights, was hesitant to mention her experience, lest she be thought of as less than sane.

Another participant in the evening reported that on subsequent occasions when she and her husband went camping, her husband (who was not at the evening) would see one of the figures watching over her at night as she slept. His description matched that given on the evening of a specific type of "Gray" appearance of which he was unaware at the time … (a being in a long dark cloak and hat, covering their features – an elder of that race).

In her book, Judy Carroll explains the feeling of paralysis that often accompanies an experience of being taken on board a ship. She says that as our natural responses are fear and panic, we are "restrained" so as to avoid the dangers of lashing out and doing damage to ourselves or the ETs. Our memory of the events is usually removed so as to avoid trauma; however some have glimpses or memories of these experiences.

Another race that has had some interaction with the Earth is that from the Pleiades. Their technologies are said to be thousands of years ahead of our own, and in time terms, they are said to be our future selves, back to assist us to get it right and not make the terrible evolutionary mistakes we are shaping up to. There are several books of teachings from the

Pleiadians channelled by Barbara Marciniak (*Bringers of the Dawn, Earth–Pleiadian Keys to the Living Library, Family of Light*) and Barbara Hand Clow (*The Pleiadian Agenda*). These offer some very interesting insights into dimensions greater than our own for those not afraid to have their ways of thought challenged and expanded.

An interesting point (as we have again touched on the concept of dimensions): These races exist at vibrational *rates* that are different than our own. Many reporting sightings have mentioned that ships are sometimes seen to appear or disappear suddenly. The explanation I have read for this is that when the space-craft's vibrational rate is stepped up or down it becomes invisible or otherwise to the human range of perception, seeming to suddenly disappear, or appear.

As mentioned earlier, other races that interact with the earth have agendas that are more warlike, or which continue to try and hold us in slavery and ignorance of our real place in the intergalactic community. These races seem mostly associated with the "Reptilian" species (like that depicted in the old TV series *V*). It is said that it is their involvement in our affairs that creates the senseless grabs for power and money which dominate world affairs and impede our ability to create harmony and peace on this planet. As stated, it could be seen that an age-old battle for supremacy is taking place right here in our midst, but that we are, on the whole, oblivious to it and have been stupefied into non-action by our own need to make ends meet and live our lives from day to day.

When you look at the craziness with which the world is run, it doesn't seem so hard to grasp that we are indeed somehow blinded to the massive, high level agendas of power, money, health treatments and weaponry that are being carried out right under our noses.

Just take a look at the best solutions this world has to offer and ask yourself, given what we know CAN be done, why positive change is just not happening as easily or quickly as it could or should.

Overall, we are warned not to make assumptions about the agendas of the various space brethren, but to *feel with our own hearts and emotions* whether they are acting in our best interests or not. There is suggestion that those who purport to come and "save" and lead us may well ultimately be binding us into more restrictions and limitations. Individual discernment is said to be the key to our own best interests.

THE LAW OF ATTRACTION

WE TOUCHED ON the topics of dimensions, vibration and reality in earlier chapters, but it is in the Law of Attraction that these concepts really come together. Many have written about this Universal law, including Quantum Physicists, but it seems we are mostly oblivious to this important principle at work in our lives.

In short, the law is this: ***"That which we think about and resonate within us is what we attract to ourselves."***

In other words, we are constantly attracting to ourselves experiences in life which are the out-workings of the thoughts and emotions that we hold within us and express to ourselves and others repeatedly.

This occurs because "like attracts like". Our vibration will draw to us experiences and people of like vibration … mirrors, if you wish, of our thoughts and feelings.

Now I am not here to prove this principle to you or to argue with you that you must believe it. There are plenty of others who have written and spoken extensively on the subject for your reference. I am merely drawing your attention to what is widely described as a physical law of the Universe, which can help you both to understand your life's experiences and ultimately to shape and control them.

The best explanation I have seen is contained in the DVD movie *The Secret*, produced by Prime Time Productions and available for purchase on the Web (use a Google search to find it). In it you will see succinct descriptions of how the law works and applies itself in our lives. This movie is a must see for anyone interested in the topic, as it uplifts, informs and provides a good "how to" guide for the viewer.

In the meantime, though, the crux of the Law of Attraction is that we are constantly creating our lives, whether consciously or unconsciously, by the vibrations we hold and project.

This applies to the things we consciously attract as well as those things that are stored in our subconscious, that we may not be aware of attracting. How many times have you noticed a friend or yourself going through almost the same scenario time and time again? Same issue, different players? We can say, 'I didn't ASK for this!' but on some level, sure as eggs, we did.

Have you noticed for instance, that people who are fearful of being "ripped off" and act overly cautiously, will tend to be justified in their belief, because there will always be someone waiting to take advantage of them; while someone who is more easy-going seems unaffected by such situations?

Or someone who "doesn't want to know" things outside of their set views, will tend to have hearing or vision impairment or degeneration?

A person who is on the whole optimistic and happy will tend to attract more things to be happy about and will even be able to interpret seemingly negative experiences in a better light, so that they benefit overall in the long run. It is more than just a pat "positive thinking" regime, it is a basic principle of how things are created in our lives. We are doing it all the time, whether consciously or by accident, so the sooner we grasp this principle and learn to work with it, the better things can be.

Many patterns of thought, belief and emotion are learned or programmed into us at an early age. A child who is abused by their parents learns to equate such abuse with receiving attention or love and then later in life, if this pattern is not dealt with, will attract a partner or others who treat them similarly, time and time again.

The healing modalities mentioned in earlier chapters give us tools to address the patterns we hold which are creating realities that we do not wish to keep repeating and as such are invaluable in our quest to evolve.

Our attitude to money, usually its scarcity, is a classic programme that we learn early in life. 'Money doesn't grow on trees!' we are told, and for most of us, it is indeed a hard thing to accumulate enough to scratch together a comfortable life. Yet for those who are free of this belief, millions of dollars come to them almost effortlessly! You only have to look at the price of luxury items in the marketplace to realize there are many who have no problem affording properties, cars and other things that the majority of us could not imagine affording.

The key to the law of attraction is to start imagining! Begin by visualizing yourself living the life and having the things and the feelings that you truly desire! It is in the mind's ability to conceive these things that the seeds of creation lie. If we don't even envision that we can have it, be it, or do it, we will not be able to attract it.

By holding a picture in our mind's eye we begin to attract it. By feeling the gratitude and joy of knowing it can and will come to us, the energies of our Universe respond by bringing that thing or that feeling to us. We must then be open to receiving it when we feel the impulse to act and bring it into reality. This is not just some whimsical idea. It has now been proven by Quantum Physicists to be the way things work.

Ignore science if you wish, but it will continue to be working this way whether you are conscious of it or not!

Being aware of this Law of Attraction allows us to consciously create our wildest dreams and our most treasured desires. Beware though! If what we create is done with malice or destructive intent towards others, we will also ultimately be drawing such "bad karma" to ourselves, so it is wise to act and create with kindness and love!

As the good book says, "Ask and ye shall receive". It is that simple. Our greatest difficulty is usually in holding the faith long enough and staying out of our own way so as to allow the thing we ask for to make its way to us.

Referred to earlier in this book are the writings of author Florence Scovel Shinn, who has eloquently and simply enlarged on the workings of this law. Her book *The Game of Life and How to Play It* is certainly worth a look at to understand this principle more easily.

There is also an old saying, "When the student is ready the Master will appear", which illustrates how, when information is sought genuinely by one who wants to learn more, the right person will cross their path, with the answers or guidance they need. Alternatively a book, article or other form of information may coincidentally become available (to the extent that a book may fall open at exactly the right page!!) when information is sought. Be open to seeing the workings of this principle in your life and you will notice any number of examples where it has already come into play for you!

SO WHAT ABOUT GOD?

THE LAW OF Attraction fits hand-in-hand with what might be termed a more enlightened, Spiritual view of Who, or What God is. In speaking of God, I am referring to that all-encompassing central Creative Source from which all things originated. Different religions have many names for the concept of God and some have many lesser gods to whom they appeal for intercession, but for the purpose of this chapter, I am referring to that which is the Source of All Things ... whatever name (or whichever gender) you may wish to attribute to it.

Stuck in our limited dimensional reality, we of course cannot hope to understand the fullness of the Infinite Creative Force with our minds alone. Our senses must be employed in order to *feel* (more so than trying to mentally grasp) that which He (and She) is. God is endless, all powerful and present in all places and things. There is nothing that is NOT of God's creation, or to put it another way nothing exists "outside of God". As such *WE TOO, ARE GOD* made manifest, split into individual units of consciousness, experiencing Himself in Infinite variations. Neale Donald Walsch, author of the bestselling series of books called *Conversations with God,* wrote:

> *"You are always immersed in the Divine. You are immersed in it right now. Indeed, you are it. You are Divinity, immersed in Divinity, expressing Itself as the Individuated Aspect of Divinity known as You."*

In this way we could see that everyone and everything we meet is in fact another aspect of ourselves, we all being parts of God's consciousness, interacting with each other. Walsch's works are recommended reading for those wishing to explore this viewpoint more fully.

The ancient Mayan Indian culture had a greeting for each other when they would meet. Where we might say '*How do you do?*' or even '*Hey*', they would say: '*In Lak'ech Ala K'in*' which roughly translated means '*I am another yourself*'. What a wonderful reminder of the greater reality that surrounds us always. As you can see, or at least imagine, if we could all grasp and apply this concept in our daily lives, what a difference it would make to our levels of love, concern, forgiveness and the like for others that we deal with. If we all saw ourselves as connected within the greatness of All That Is, we would have a different view, perhaps, of wars, hatred, hunger and so on. We might even start treating each other as we would want to be treated ourselves! (Doesn't that sound familiar?) '*That which you do to the least of my brothers, you do unto ME.*'

The creative power described in the previous chapter on "The Law of Attraction" can, in this light be seen as God's manifesting ability, borne out through each of us. We are each of us creating our lives using the same creative force (albeit stepped down) as God. We might see more clearly then, that it is for US to create Heaven on Earth with our own intentions, thoughts, words and deeds. The power lies within, which is why we are always told to "look inside ourselves".

In a previous chapter, I spoke about religions and how devout members of churches may well believe the above to be some form of blasphemy, but as I said earlier, those holding this view are invited to look within their own hearts and FEEL for themselves if what has been expressed here sits with their own conscience and their own consciousness. In truth, I personally cannot believe in a God who goes around smiting and invoking fear, mistrust or divisiveness ... one who would not be tolerant of a variety of viewpoints within His Infinite Creation. Believe what you will, but let it be what your heart feels happy and right with, not what you are told that you must believe in, even against your own instincts ... and that goes for what I say too!

EARTH CHANGES & OUR FUTURE

THERE HAS BEEN quite a lot written about the changes that our Earth is going through in these times and what they are all about. Some people are fearfully expecting great cataclysms, earthquakes and natural disasters. Global warming is a very real topic of concern, let alone the notion of asteroids crashing into our planet, or nuclear destruction.

The key, perhaps, to understanding these changes, is in realizing that the consciousness of this planet and all of us upon it is evolving. No longer do we believe the Earth is flat or that the Sun revolves around it. We have grown in our understandings of things. We are beginning to grasp our part in creating the scenarios around ourselves.

In these times, our understanding of our own consciousness is being enlarged. We are coming to realize that we are greater beings than just the flesh and blood bodies and minds we were born with. We are seeing glimpses of our

Eternal, Divine and extra-dimensional existence. We are said to be reintegrating the 12 strands of DNA which were part of our original make-up, but lost in previous eons, causing extreme limitation in our ability to perceive our true nature and fullness.

As young adults move out of home and create new lives for themselves, our ways of thinking are becoming more unlimited, expanding out to new horizons and breaking free of the constricting belief structures we were brought up to operate within.

Similarly, our Earth is changing and adjusting to reflect our shifts in consciousness. This can happen by cataclysm, if we are unwilling to expand ourselves voluntarily and need to be pushed, or it can happen more gently and smoothly, if our understandings can expand in a calmer way. As the human race evolves to understand the connections between all things, the shifts are echoed in the Earth's movements.

There is a measurement of the Earth's vibrational rate, or "heartbeat" as it is sometimes described, known as the Schumann Resonance. This frequency was in preceding times steady at 7.83 Hz. In more recent years, it has increased to as high as 12 and 13 Hz. It is an indication that the vibrational rate on this planet is rising – that the speed at which the Earth and all of us on it resonate is increasing.

It means that our bodies and our thoughts are evolving and changing to take in new parameters, views and understandings of what we are all about ... the true nature of our existence in these three dimensions and beyond. You only have to take an inexpert look at the new scientific breakthroughs such as "String Theory" and "M Theory" to see that things are far more than they seem.

Ancient civilizations have written about this period in the

Earth's evolution and have made prophecies about the times to come. The Ancient Mayans were known as the Timekeepers of our Galaxy. They plotted calendars that accurately calculated planetary movements and epochs over hundreds of thousands of years. They are considered to have had amazing mathematical, astronomical and prophetic abilities, borne out through the accuracy of their time-keeping system. Now here's the rub: their calendar ends on the 21st December, 2012.

The end of the Mayan Calendar has been debated by many and it is said by some to mark the end of the world, but more so, it is considered that it marks a defined change in our grasp of the nature of reality in this dimension. Time, as we know it, may cease to exist on this plane.

There is a phenomenon known as the Photon Band, which is comprised (simplistically), of a band of higher vibrational energy that stretches through space and which our Earth enters and exits in its rotation around our Sun. The Sun, in turn, is moving deeper into the Band, as it rotates around a greater, central Sun. The upshot of all this movement is that, whereas our Earth, prior to 1987, never entered this Photon Band, and existed in what is known as "Galactic Night", it is now moving into the Band increasingly at certain times of each year and by the predicted 2012 date, both the Earth and the Sun will be wholly positioned within the Photon Band.

The effects of this positioning are said to be the increasing vibration of the planet and all matter upon her, as evidenced by the Schumann Resonance Frequency referred to earlier.

In short, the Photon Band and our increasing frequency are causing us to break out of old constricting thought structures and understandings about who we are and what we are and how this whole Universe thing works.

It is thought that by the time we are living fully within the influence of this Photon Band (the predicted Mayan Calendar date in 2012), we will have a totally different grasp of the concepts of time and consciousness, such that the lives we will be living will bear little if any resemblance to our state of being now. Many fear they will not be able to make the leaps of consciousness necessary to move into our future in this way, but we should bear in mind that this rising level of consciousness surrounds and fills us as it resonates our Planet and we are borne along and lifted with it, so to speak.

Mass disasters are said, in this context, to be the Earth's adjustment to these new ways and along with that, the departure of those souls who have chosen not to make this adjustment on Earth at this time and who are thus leaving for other dimensions.

The trick to moving with the flow is to allow old concepts and limited views to change as they no longer "fit" with our truths. To recognize where we are clinging to our tunnel vision and gently let it go, in favour of a wider and deeper understanding of the true reality around us, including (as a basic starting point) the kind of concepts written of in this book.

Perhaps considering the concept of crop circles gives us a good example of this type of expansion of awareness. Hopefully you are at least a little familiar with crop circles and may have seen pictures of these huge graphic "designs" imprinted into fields around the world. It is usually the case that people find them perplexing and decide to write them off as hoaxes, as they do not fit any other paradigm of thought that we have. This may be a convenient means of mentally coping with such a phenomenon, but it really is not satisfactory if you have any interest in the true situation.

If you research crop circles in any depth, you will find that they simply are NOT hoaxes (except the few very uncharacteristic attempts that ARE) and that they have evolved over the years into more and more intricate and mathematically complex diagrams of design perfection and knowledge.

The means by which they have been created is something of a mystery, but points towards an extra-dimensional source. Indeed, due to certain anomalies in the way plant stalks are bent and the energies found in and around them, it is pretty clear that normal human endeavour could not have formed these circles. Interestingly, the researchers of this topic have noted a certain interactive quality in the designs, newly created crop circles providing pictographic "replies" to questions posed, from time to time, by the researchers in the course of their work. There are books and documentary movies available to those wanting to know more. One movie which provides a good overview on this topic is entitled "Star Dreams" released in 2007 by the Spiritual Cinema Inc (written and directed by Robert L. Nichol). Before dismissing the phenomenon, it is worth watching and considering what experts in this field have to say, with an open mind.

The human mind finds it hard to grasp these concepts and therefore puts them into the "too hard" box, going about its normal day's activities, oblivious to the depth of realness being echoed in this phenomenon. The kind of consciousness expansion that we are talking about here is one where, for starters, we even *acknowledge* that crop circles are very real and then realize that the truth about them is outside of our third dimensional grasp and exists in levels of reality we do not presently understand. It is said, for instance, that the crop circles may be that part of a larger dimensional occurrence that we only see a three dimensional "imprint" of at our level. (Much like a two dimensional flat surface cannot recognize a cube that intersects it.)

There is no doubt that the circles are not random, nor are they fake, but that they are created by some intelligent, interactive source. Their purpose, it seems, is *at least* to awaken our senses to there being more "out there" than we can perceive or understand.

In these times on Earth we are encouraged to think outside of the square we live in. It need not be scary. It need not be too hard. It is said that on a Spiritual level we all chose to be born into this lifetime here and now so as to witness and take part in this amazing period of evolution in the Earth's history. We are invited to step up to the plate, so to speak, and play our parts in this unstoppable tide.

No doubt we are heading for interesting times and we are encouraged to expand and enjoy greater realities as they present themselves to us in coming days, months and years. It may be that we are suddenly faced with a new reality, or that over time it will creep into our awareness gradually, but the expansion is afoot and will continue!

Look out for your intuition as it speaks to you. Follow your heart's guidance, rather than the "mob rules" mentality. Recognize your uniqueness and be kind and loving towards your own needs, not just to those of others. In time, you will see glimpses of your eternal nature and your connection with the Divine Source. Most of all, HAVE FUN! You are here to create as fulfilling a lifetime experience for yourself as you can. No one else can do it for you.

You are the Captain of your own vessel.
May your seas be smooth and your journey, amazing!